Glasgow's West End walks

Walks (or cycles) in and near the west end area of Glasgow making use of the "green places" of woodland, river & canal paths, and parks

An Exploreourworld "mini-guide"

Copyright Yvonne Carroll 2020

Contents

INTRODUCTION 3

1.   The Kelvin Way loop - from Maryhill Locks to Kelvingrove Park, coming back via Ashton Lane and the Botanic gardens and exploring suggested places of interest in the "west end" along the way (approx 6 miles return) 6

2.   A circular walk along the Kelvin Way into Dawsholm Park and Cairnhill Woods, coming back along the Forth & Clyde canal path (approx 5 miles) 19

3.   A circular walk from Maryhill Locks to the Western Necropolis, Possil Marsh and back along the Forth & Clyde canal path (approx 5.5 miles) 28

4.   Return walk or cycle from Maryhill Locks along the Forth & Clyde canal path to the Stables pub near Kirkintilloch (approx 13 miles return)..................................34

5.   The Drumchapel Way – a circular walk mostly through woodland, with some spectacular views over the city and beyond (approx 4.5 miles)....................................39

6.   Maryhill Locks to Speirs Wharf and *Claypits Local Nature Reserve at Hamilton Hill (approx. 6 miles return)...47

APPENDIX (Temporary diversion in place on a section of Walk 6)..55

INTRODUCTION

Living where Kelvindale and Maryhill meet, near the Maryhill Locks and the Kelvin Walkway at the bottom of "the Butney" (Cowal Road), we are very well placed for walks in and near the west end of Glasgow. With the lockdown of 2020, we have spent even more time exploring the area on foot, which has inspired the writing of this mini guide book.

It's easy to get used to getting in the car and heading further afield for leisure/walks or to keep to the same routine (the first walk described is our "usual" west end walk).

However, the lockdown made us start to look for alternatives, which has led us to discover new walks and to rediscover some old ones that we had either forgotten about or just never do any more (usually because there are no pubs to stop at!)

The following six walks either start at the River Kelvin Walkway or at Maryhill Locks, both of which are accessible off the main road outside of our estate (Cowal Road, which leads up the hill and on to Maryhill

Road). Each walk is a *minimum* of two hours duration at an easy pace.

If you live close to either the canal path or the Kelvin Walkway, you can join them at your closest entry point and use this to either lengthen or shorten your walk, depending on the direction travelled.

The walks are pretty easy to follow, however, for anyone with a smartphone, you can download "What3Words" for free. This is used to pinpoint a location to within 3 square metres.

For those using this app, at the end of each walk description, we have listed the 3Words for the start/end point and any places en route that might be just a little hard to find.

Because the locations where each walk starts and ends are so close, any of the walks can be put together to make a longer walk. We have included some suggestions for this and/or optional side trips in italics.

All of the walks described are also suitable for bicycles, so they can be done as either a walk or a cycle.

This guide should be ideal for tourists visiting the west end, anyone new to the area and locals looking for nearby places to explore.

We hope you enjoy the walks and the photographs and find this guide useful.

Have fun exploring!

1. **The Kelvin Way loop - from Maryhill Locks to Kelvingrove Park, coming back via Ashton Lane and the Botanic gardens and exploring suggested places of interest in the "west end" along the way (approx 6 miles return)**

Start on the canal path at Maryhill Locks and head downhill until you see the turnoff for the Kelvin Walkway on your left. The path takes a couple of zig-zags downhill and then you are on the Kelvin Walkway. The walkway follows the River Kelvin right into, and through, Kelvingrove Park (it eventually enters the River Clyde at the Riverside Museum).

It's a beautiful walk in all seasons and was our "go-to" weekend jaunt until the lockdown (when we then started to look for some alternatives for a bit of variety).

Being mostly flat, it is a popular and easy route for both walkers and cyclists.

PHOTO: The Kelvin Walkway near Maryhill

Although it is paved, we would recommend wellies in or after any heavy rain as small parts can get flooded, especially after the second bridge that crosses the river just before the Botanic Gardens.

For those interested in history, a little way after the part of the walkway that follows adjacent to the Botanic Gardens, you will pass the ruins of the North Woodside flint mill.

PHOTO: The Kelvin Walkway looking back to the Queen Margaret Bridge

PHOTO: The Kelvin Walkway nearing the Woodside Flint Mill ruins

We would recommend a refreshment stop at Inn Deep on a sunny day should you be lucky enough to get one of their outside tables next to the river.

PHOTO: Having a beer outside Inn Deep

Failing that, take a short diversion up the stairs and head to Bank Street Bar & Kitchen five minutes' walk away (follow the road round to the left from the top of the stairs to Otago Street and turn left when you reach it, then take a right onto Glasgow Street and your next left onto Bank Street). It's one of our regular haunts for lunch. Being near the university it's popular with students and the food and drinks they serve are both good and cheap – we always have the "pint and pakora for £5" and usually a pizza. The pakora (and especially the dip that comes with it) is fabulous!

If you go to Bank Street, you can either head back to the stairs to continue on the walkway past Inn Deep and into Kelvingrove Park, or you can cross the road diagonally and head down Gibson Street to the park (a quicker option).

Kelvingrove Park is lovely for a walk around, and they also have some picnic tables set up to BBQ on should that appeal. There are play areas for the kids, lots of pathways to explore and plenty of good spots to rest and soak up some sun. The park continues across the main road (the Kelvin Way).

PHOTO: Looking over Kelvingrove pond to Glasgow university tower

From here you can do a few things:

A) walk along Kelvin Way and turn left up University Avenue and pop in to explore the beautiful University grounds and the Hunterian Museum
B) continue through the park towards Argyll Street and then do almost a U-turn into the University grounds and explore as above

C) visit our wonderful Kelvingrove Art Gallery & Museum (free to enter, although donations are appreciated)

PHOTO: The main entrance to the Kelvingrove Museum & Art Gallery

If you chose to visit the museum, you may want to either have a refreshment in the museum cafe or pop across the road to Brewdog and sample some of their popular craft beers (you can get a "beer flight" where you sample a third of a pint of four different beers).

PHOTO: Trying a beer flight in Brewdog

Whichever of the above options you have chosen; your next stop is Glasgow University.

PHOTO: The Cloisters at Glasgow University

Both the grounds of the university, especially around the Cloisters, and the Hunterian Museum are great for passing an hour or so.

Head out of the University grounds and onto University Avenue. Cross the road and take a right along University Gardens. Cut down the lane on the left that passes Brel's beer garden and into Ashton Lane.

PHOTO: A quiet Ashton Lane during the 2020 lockdown

Ashton Lane is the hub of the west end's pub and restaurant scene. Our recommendations for food would be Brel (their cheese and chocolate fondues are fabulous), the Ashoka and the Ubiquitous Chip, which has a great reputation but is a little pricier.

For beer gardens, our favourites are the ones at Brel and Jinty's. It is worth mentioning that at the time of writing Jinty's is cash only, however you will get your drink in a glass at Jinty's, whereas Brel will give you a plastic cup...

In winter, the "Chip" is our favourite choice as it has a log fire. (The "Chip" is the pub part of the Ubiquitous Chip).

PHOTO: Jinty's beer garden

Walking on to Byres Road after Ashton Lane, there are many more pubs and restaurants. Our favourite for food is Cafe Andaluz(it's just off Byres Road on Cresswell Lane). They do fantastic Spanish tapas.

For drinks on Byres Road, our favourite is BeGin, which is owned by the Grosvenor Hotel. They do table service, which is a nice touch, and tend to be quieter than many of the other pubs. Another nice pub is Oran Mor (the former Kelvinside Parish Church). This is very popular for those who like things to be livelier – they have (among other things) two bars, a nightclub, restaurant, theatre and live entertainment.

At the end of Byres Road, and crossing Great Western Road, you get to the entrance of the Botanic Gardens. These gardens are always really stunning; the council regularly change the flower beds as the season's change, so there are always lots of colours. The "hot houses" (as we called them as kids) are wonderful too. In summer the gardens get busy, as people come out to enjoy them and to sunbathe or have a picnic. There is a cafe, normally open till around 4 or 5 pm, if you need refreshment.

PHOTO: Rainbow over the Botanic Gardens

Come out the far end of the gardens and turn right down the hill to rejoin the Kelvin Walkway and trace your route back.

What3Words

Start/end point (Maryhill Locks) – lame.saving.mouse

The turnoff from the canal path onto the Kelvin Walkway – couple.wink.slowly

Inn Deep – pasta.gear.agreed

Bank Street Bar & Kitchen – wash.slate.token

Kelvingrove Museum & Art Gallery front entrance – comic.deaf.packet

Brewdog – squad.hired.dusty

University entrance from Argyll Street / Dumbarton Road – purely.trunk.moon

University entrance/exit from University Avenue – fast.spice.race

Turnoff past Brel's beer garden – takes.plants.dozed

Ashton Lane (coming from the path past Brel) – chained.sock.talked

Cafe Andaluz – monks.owls.decide

BeGin – chair.puddles.supply

Oran Mor – paused.twigs.weedy

Botanic Gardens entrance – modes.usual.cans

Botanic Gardens exit (turn right and head downhill to rejoin the walkway) – human.hulk.lion

2. A circular walk along the Kelvin Way into Dawsholm Park and Cairnhill Woods, coming back along the Forth & Clyde canal path (approx 5 miles)

Start this walk by joining the Kelvin Way at the bottom of Cowal Road (you can join on either side of the road). This time you are taking the Kelvin Walkway in the other direction towards Garscube Estate and Bearsden.

PHOTO: Looking along the Kelvin Walkway from Cowal Road

You will only be on the walkway for about half a mile when you will see the signpost for Dawsholm Park (walking over the bridge to your left). Staying on the walkway will take you into Garscube Estate.

SIDE TRIP / ALTERNATIVE ROUTE: Heading into Garscube Estate is an alternative to Dawsholm Park, as both come out more or less opposite Cairnhill Woods (if you head out of Garscube via the Vet School). Garscube Estate is part of Glasgow University and is vast (nearly as big as Dawsholm Park). It's also a lovely place for a walk. You can take the main Kelvin Walkway path in or drop on to the riverside path to access it (the latter can get muddy in places after rain).

PHOTO: The grounds of Garscube Estate

I teach classes at the Sports Complex there and had no idea just how beautiful and vast the grounds were until we started looking for new places to exercise during the lockdown. We would highly recommend this as either a side trip (i.e. head back to Dawsholm Park afterwards) or an alternative to Daswholm if you are doing this walk a second time.

Once in Dawsholm Park, there is a multitude of footpaths that cover the park. You could make several visits and discover new routes each time. Just make sure you head out of the main entrance at Ilay Road to then cross the Switchback into Cairnhill Woods to continue on this route.

Make sure you take some time in the park to look for the resident parakeets! They are beautiful birds, which apparently originated in Victoria Park. We have found the best place to spot them is in the trees on the path next to the small pond (keeping the pond on your left as you are walking through the park). If you have taken the high path along the river, then you have to drop down away from the river at the first opportunity.

PHOTO: A parakeet in Dawsholm Park

There are undoubtedly other good places in the park where you can spot the parakeets, but this one works best for us.

Exiting the park onto Ilay Road, continue forward no more than 200 metres to the Switchback (Bearsden Road) and cross carefully. The path into Cairnhill Woods is directly opposite the spot where Ilay Rpad meets the Switchback.

The first section of Cairnhill Woods is mainly a thin, narrow strip of woodland with the houses of Henderland Road to your right and Maxwell Avenue to your left backing onto it. The second section is a little wider and substantially bigger. You come out at

Henderland Road and cross over to access the second section of woods.

I used to play there when I was a kid. At that time we called them the Bluebell Woods as they were carpeted in bluebells in the Spring. I had forgotten all about them until we rediscovered them during our lockdown search for new local walks.

The bluebells are a little sparse now, but even so, it is probably the best place to see them in the west end of Glasgow. There are also several wood carvings, mostly of various animals (bears, owl, deer etc), to be found throughout the woods, so it's a great place for kids as well as adults.

PHOTO: Wood carvings in Cairnhill Woods

PHOTO: Path through Cairnhill Woods in Spring

On this walk, you are going to exit about half-way through the second section of woods and back onto Henderland Road, but if you have time then continue on the woodland path before exiting, as it makes a circular loop back to the exit path.

When you exit follow the signs for Westerton train station. You can take the path down past Westerton Primary School and on to Maxwell Avenue, and then take a left to head to the train station, which is across the road on your right.

At the train station cross the bridge over the railway and the next bridge over the canal, then join the canal path for the final part of the walk along the Forth & Clyde canal. For refreshments stop at Lock 27 and enjoy their outdoor canal-side seating. The "Lock" serves pub-style food as well as drinks and is a great place to stop and enjoy a cold drink and some sunshine on a summer's day.

PHOTO: Looking up the canal path towards Lock 27

You can then either walk on to Maryhill Locks to finish or turn off at the zig-zags which lead down to the Kelvin Walkway. At the bottom of the zig-zags make a right turn and a short distance on you will be back to where you started the walk where you can exit back onto Cowal Road.

What3Words

Start/end point (the turnoff from Cowal road to the Kelvin Walkway) – coins.marked.care

Kelvin Walkway (joining point after Cowal Road – turn right at the bottom of the steps) – rods.saves.shave

Dawsholm Park turnoff – teach.strut.hill

Where we saw the parakeets (approx) – blues.fuel.hiking

Dawsholm Park exit – dress.trains.decide

Garscube Estate exit – starts.atomic.robe

Cairnhill Woods entrance – drove.hung.transmitted

Cairnhill Woods exit for heading to the canal path – flames.latest.issued

Westerton train station (bridge over the railway) – moved.gears.watch

Canal path joining point – trend.focal.wiring

Maryhill Locks (optional end point, and start point for linking to walks 1, 3, 4 & 6) - lame.saving.mouse

3. A circular walk from Maryhill Locks to the Western Necropolis, Possil Marsh and back along the Forth & Clyde canal path (approx 5.5 miles)

The start of this walk goes through urban areas for approximately one mile. We have written it this way as we prefer a circular walk where possible.

ALTERNATIVE (NON-CIRCULAR) ROUTE AVOIDING URBAN AREAS: The only way to avoid the urban area is to make a longer return trip via the canal path to Possil Marsh, then cross over Balmore Road to the Western Necropolis (which adjoins Lambhill and St Kentigern's Cemeteries – you will be coming in at Lambhill Cemetery) and return once again via Possil Marsh and the canal path.

From Maryhill Locks, cross Maryhill Road at the traffic lights near Feng Huang (Chinese takeaway). Take the path up the side of the takeaway keeping it on your left, turn left and then right onto Duncruin Street. Head up Duncruin Street until you get to Sandbank Street. Turn left onto Sandbank Street and then a prompt first right onto Thornton Street. In less than

100 metres, take a left onto Knowetap Street. As you follow this street round to the right, stop to admire the far-reaching views on your left. On a clear day, you can see Dumgoyne Hill and Ben Lomond.

PHOTO: Far-reaching views from the grassy area on Knowtap Street

At the end of Knowetap Street, you are nearly there. Take a left onto Cadder Road and when Cadder Road branches left, keep right (looks like straight) on Tresta Road for around 150 metres to then enter the Western Necropolis / Glasgow Crematorium.

With the other two cemeteries adjacent to the Western Necropolis, this gives you plenty of scope for walking or cycling. There are several paths within the grounds, but whichever ones you take, try at some point to head up to the top of the hill for great views over the city and out to the countryside.

PHOTO: Headstones within the Western Necropolis

PHOTO: Looking over the city from the Western Necropolis

Once you have finished exploring, you can exit at Lambhill Cemetery and carefully cross Balmore Road to join the path round Possil Marsh. Just where you join this path, after crossing Balmore Road, you have the option to take the rough "path" down to Possil Loch, then back to rejoin the main path around Possil Marsh.

Possil Marsh is very popular for bird watching and is one of my late father's old haunts.

The final part of this walk is along the Forth & Clyde canal path, which you reach from the path around Possil Marsh. Once you have joined the canal path, watch out for the sign for the viewpoint which is worth checking out and only a very short walk from the path.

PHOTO: Possil Marsh nature reserve

Along the canal, you can stop for refreshments at Lambhill Stables, just before the path heads under Balmore Road. This is the only opportunity before you finish the walk. As you approach the Stockingfield Junction near Lochburn Road, make sure you take the right fork to come off the canal path, go under the bridge (which the canal flows over) and then immediately take the path on your left (or the steps opposite – on the other side of the road) to come back up onto the canal path ready to head towards Maryhill Locks. The canal would have been on your left, now it is on your right.

Finish the walk back at Maryhill Locks.

What3Words

Start/end point (Maryhill Locks at Maryhill Road) – tanks.slap.shirt

Alternative (non-circular) Start/end point if avoiding urban areas (Maryhill Locks on the canal path) - lame.saving.mouse

Feng Huang (path) – aura.weeks.proven

Western Necropolis entrance – laptop.pits.vibrate

Possil Marsh footpath entrance (opposite Lambill Cemetery exit) – repair.divisions.begun

Joining the canal path – ears.estate.zebra

Viewpoint – trying.judges.dizzy

Lambhill Stables – retain.note.ducks

Stockingfield Junction exit off the canal path (canal was on your left) – pinch.sling.react

Stockingfield Junction rejoining the canal path (keep the canal on your right now) – spits.joins.farms (this is easiest if you are cycling, however you can also take the path with the steps which is directly opposite on the other side of the road – milk.smiled.shovels)

4. Return walk or cycle from Maryhill Locks along the Forth & Clyde canal path to the Stables pub near Kirkintilloch (approx 13 miles return)

This route we prefer to do as a cycle as it makes for a pretty lengthy walk. We do this one on a nice warm sunny day, planning to arrive at the Stables around lunchtime so we can sit out in their garden to have some lunch in the sun.

It's a popular place on a sunny day and there can sometimes be quite a wait at the bar to order (there is no table service if you sit outside, you have to go in to order, bring your own drinks out and then your meal will be brought out when it's ready).

The food can be excellent, the pizzas in particular and it is one of our favourite places to go for a weekend lunch in good weather.

PHOTO: Having a drink in the sun at the Stables

Join the canal path at Maryhill Locks with the canal on your left side and remember to come off at the Stockingfield Junction near Lochburn Road to pass under the bridge and rejoin with the canal now on your right side. Other than that, the route is straightforward and easy to follow, keeping on the canal path all the way to the Stables. It's a good and mostly level path, subject to just the odd puddle after heavy rain.

PHOTO: The canal path on the way to the Stables

PHOTO: A heron on the canal

Sometimes instead of cycling, we drive to Cadder Wharf and then go to the Stables in our inflatable canoe (from Cadder Wharf this is only around 3 miles return).

For keen cyclists, but too far for walkers, you can make a full day trip by continuing along the canal path for approximately another 16 miles to the Falkirk Wheel, a rotating boat lift (we have not cycled this far, it is on our list of things to do!)

Roughly another 4.5 miles, also along the canal path, will take you to the famous Kelpies, one of the most photographed sculptures in Scotland, created to pay homage to the working horses that used to pull the barges along the canals.

Return is along the same route.

SUGGESTED ADD-ON: This trip could easily be added on route 3 by either -

A) Making a side trip to Possil Marsh and the Western Necropolis (and then coming back on to the canal path to avoid using the roads) or

B) By heading back to Maryhill Locks following route 3 in reverse via Possil Marsh, Western Necropolis and through the urban areas. The latter would involve some cycling on the roads.

<u>What3Words</u>

Start/end point (Maryhill Locks) – lame.saving.mouse

Stockingfield Junction exit off the canal path (the canal was on your left) – loaded.spits.shelf (currently closed during development work) OR analogy.lasts.porch (this involves steps)

Stockingfield Junction rejoining the canal path (the canal is now on your right) – belt.paying.glue

Stables pub (turnoff) – minute.cone.second

5. The Drumchapel Way – a circular walk mostly through woodland, with some spectacular views over the city and beyond (approx 4.5 miles)

For the purpose of this book, the walk starts and ends at the junction of Canniesburn Road and Kinfauns Drive (opposite the Scotmid Co-op). *This makes it pretty easy to link on to route 2 with only about half a mile through urban areas between the walks.*

Although the Drumchapel Way is a circular route, we felt that it would have been nicer done as a return walk going through Garscadden Woods East & West to Cleddans Burn and then looping back the same way. There is an opportunity to come back on different paths within some areas of the woods and to make a loop out of the high and low path at Cleddans Burn.

However, as it is a circular route, I will describe it in this way. It's worth doing once as a circular route, and then you can decide what you want to do on any subsequent visits.

TO LINK THIS WALK TO CAIRNHILL WOODS (ROUTE 2):
On the path through Cairnhill Woods go as far as you
can and take the exit that leads on to Canniesburn
Drive. Turn left, then 50 metres on, head left through
the woods again on the path that leads down to
Maxwell Avenue. Walk (or cycle) up Maxwell Avenue
and turn left on to Canniesburn Road. Follow
Canniesburn Road downhill, up, then down again to the
junction (at the traffic lights) with Kinfauns Drive (more
or less opposite the Co-op). Assuming you have walked
or cycled on the left, now cross Canniesburn Road at
the traffic lights (if you are cycling just come off and
push), and go along Kinfauns Drive (on the right) for
about 50 metres. You will see on the right a footpath
through the grass (and then through trees), this is the
path that will take you to Garscadden Woods.

Follow the path (which runs adjacent to Kinfauns Drive
for most of the way) until you get to Drummore Road,
where you cross the road and head into Garscadden
Woods East. These woods are also known locally as the
"Bluebell Woods" and rightly so. This is probably the
best place in Glasgow to see carpets of bluebells in
Spring. Not quite as good as Inchcailloch or our go-to
spots in the Lake District, but a good option if you want

to stay local. We also were lucky enough to see a roe deer in these woods.

PHOTO: The "bluebell woods" (Garscadden Woods East)

PHOTO: Roe deer in Garscadden Woods

Before you get to Garscadden Woods West, from the East woods take the path that cuts off to the right and heads uphill to the site of an old Roman fort. There are no ruins to see, but the views across the city from the top of the hill are worth the extra (short) hike. This is just past the junction on the main path where you can go straight on or left. *If you're on the lower path, the option is straight on or right, in which case turn right, then left on the main path and look out for the small path to the fort on your right-hand side after approximately 30 metres.*

Continue through Garscadden Woods West (a pretty walk, but without the abundance of bluebells) and come out near the "Church on the Hill" (which ironically isn't on a hill). You're now heading through a little bit of urban area to Cleddans Burn. You will see the water tower on the top of the hill and this is where you want to head for great views over the city and out to the countryside. There is a high path and a low path. If you plan to head back the way you came (through the Garscadden Woods) you can do both by making a loop, otherwise, we would suggest the high path for the stunning views.

PHOTO: View from the water tower in Cleddans Burn Park

When you exit Cleddans Burn Park you now have to walk about ¾ mile through urban areas. There are signposts to follow for the Drumchapel Way, but they seem to have disappeared at certain places, so taking a printed copy of the map is useful. If you don't have access to a printer, just make sure you're heading down Halgreen Avenue and that after the Antonine Primary School, you take a right and then you're next left down Hecla Avenue with Drumchapel Park now on your left-hand side. The final part of the walk, Garscadden Burn Park, heads off behind the Donald Dewar leisure centre and in front of the Linkwood Flats. The flats are high so they stand out, so if you head for them and keep them to your left, you can't go too far wrong.

PHOTO: The Drumchapel Way signs to look out for

PHOTO: The Linkwood Flats at the entrance to Garscadden Burn Park

We found the final part of the walk through Garscadden Burn Park to be rather disappointing. It's quite open and you can see over to the houses on your left. There was also quite a lot of rubbish lying about. For this reason, as mentioned earlier, we recommend doing the loop around Cleddans Burn Park using the high and low paths and heading back via the Garscadden Woods.

SUGGESTED ADD-ON: If you linked this walk with Route 2 as suggested, just follow Canniesburn Road back to Maxwell Avenue and either retrace your steps through Cairnhill Woods/Dawsholm/Kelvin Walkway or head on to the canal path at Westerton railway station to return as per Route 2.

What3Words

Start/end point (Kinfauns Drive after turning right onto it from Canniesburn Road) – sank.unique.push

Garscadden Woods East entrance – back.punchy.until

The turnoff for the path to the old Roman Fort (approx) – split.lazy.ticket

Site of the outskirts of the old Roman Fort (approx - for views of the city) – friend.photos.second

Cleddans Burn entrance (high path) – launcher.wizard.stirs

Cleddans Burn entrance (low path) – ironclad.simulates.bleat

Cleddans Burn water tower (for panoramic views) – instincts.routs.gymnasium

Garscadden Burn Park entrance (heading through urban areas to access) – crust.neon.throw

6. Maryhill Locks to Speirs Wharf and *Claypits Local Nature Reserve at Hamilton Hill (approx. 6 miles return)

*NOTE: Claypits is still under development of their walking/cycle path network, however the building of the new access bridge from Firhill has now been completed and (at the time of writing this update) the first path is now partially open. We think it will be a great place to visit once it fully opens, especially once they have the new paths and cycleways in place, so we wanted to keep it listed as part of this walk.

PLEASE READ THE APPENDIX IN CONJUNCTION WITH THIS WALK DESCRIPTION

For this walk, starting at Maryhill Locks, there is no need to come off the canal path where it splits at the Stockingfield Junction, just stay on the path signposted to Speirs Wharf (towards the city centre). For 200 metres or so after the Stockingfield Junction, keep an eye out on the other side of the canal, as we have spotted deer on this small stretch before. I would guess they live in the woods around the golf course at Ruchill.

PHOTO: Stockingfield Junction

This part of the canal is more urban than the stretch mentioned on Route 4 that goes to the Stables, however, there are still plenty of birds and wildlife. We saw some roe deer, as mentioned earlier, near the Stockingfield Junction and a pair of swans and their cygnets near Firhill. Herons are also a fairly common sight.

PHOTO: Swans and cygnets near Firhill

PHOTO: Art painted on the wall across the canal

When you arrive at Speirs Wharf, close to the city centre, there are lots of colourful canal boats.

PHOTO: Canal boats at Speirs Wharf

PHOTO: Looking over to Ocho Cafe

At Speirs Wharf, Ocho Cafe is a nice place for lunch or some refreshment. There is also a lovely spa next door should you wish to pre-book a treatment. You will be on the other side of the canal should you visit Ocho, however, you cannot continue your walk on that side as a high fence at the end of the wharf stops you from going further and also blocks off the footbridge. We are not sure if this fence is permanent, but it did look to be. You, therefore, have to make your way back approximately one kilometre along the same side of the canal that you arrived on until you reach Applecross Wharf. Here you cross the footbridge to the

Claypits entrance at Applecross Street next to the Scottish Canals office.

Go in and explore around the nature reserve looking out for the roe deer and other wildlife. Make sure you head uphill to check out the view from the top.

Until the new footpaths and bridge are built (which will allow for a loop by using different entry and exit points), you simply return the way you came and rejoin the canal path again at Applecross Wharf.

Return to Maryhill Locks to finish the walk.

PHOTO: Maryhill Locks

SIDE TRIP: On the canal path, behind Firhill Football Stadium, you can cross the canal on Firhill Road and go into Ruchill Park. Here is a photo of the bridge where you should cross.

PHOTO: More wall art under the bridge that crosses to Ruchill Park

Ruchill is a beautiful park with a vast network of paths that you could easily spend an hour or so exploring. Once inside the park, if you take the path up to the flagpole, you can enjoy extensive views over the city.

PHOTO: View over Maryhill and beyond from the flagpole in Ruchill Park

Once you have explored the park, simply exit where you came in and cross back on to the canal path to continue your journey.

<u>What3Words</u>

Start/end point (Maryhill Locks) – lame.saving.mouse

Ocho Cafe (approx) – begin.worry.stole

Entrance to Claypits Nature Reserve – rocks.boxer.spoil

Where to come off to go into Ruchill Park – shells.scores.pillow (cross over the canal here at Firhill Road)

Entrance to Ruchill Park (approx) – tonic.meal.store

APPENDIX (Temporary diversion in place on a section of Walk 6)

There is a temporary diversion in place (the notice says until summer 2022) due to the closure of a small section of the canal path during development works. This diversion affects Walk 6, not far from the start point at Maryhill Locks.

Below is a photograph of the diversion sign...

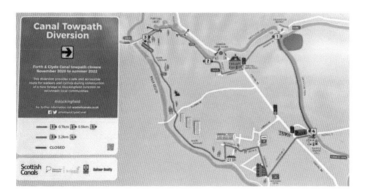

We found this a little hard to follow, so here is our description of the best options, using What3Words:

To use the suggested diversion, which takes you partly along the Kelvin Walkway – Start as in Walk 1, by heading along the Kelvin Walkway: From the canal path at Maryhill Locks, instead of heading in the direction of Speirs Wharf, head downhill and take the zig-zag path (at W3W couple.wink.slowly) onto the Kelvin Walkway (at W3W pops.chart.coats – continue ahead on the walkway at the bottom of the zig-zags). To make things easier, we would recommend that, rather than use the diversion in the above photo, come off the Kelvin Walkway when it reaches Kelvindale Road (at W3W mash.stop.engine). Instead of continuing on the walkway, turn left to stay on Kelvindale Road and keep going until it reaches Maryhill Road (cross over to the other side of Kelvindale Road at some point). Turn right onto Maryhill Road (at approx W3W error.from.avoid) and head in the direction of the town centre. Cross Maryhill Road at the pedestrian lights, and continue heading towards town. Soon you will reach the Viking Pub (at approx W3W using.live.trick), which is on the corner of Maryhill Road and Shakespeare Street. Turn left at the pub, along Shakespeare Street and past the McDonald's car park. On your right (at approx W3W maybe.descended.images) you will see the path that joins the canal path. Stay ahead and now follow the walk as described.

A quicker alternative – the diversion we chose was to start the route as described from Maryhill Locks, heading along the canal path and past the canal-side flats (on your right) towards Speirs Wharf. When you pass the flats, head off the canal path (at W3W range.knots.lived) and follow the road down past Gairbraid Parish Church to the corner of Burnhouse Street and Gairbraid Avenue (at W3W dizzy.grace.scans). The building on the corner houses Maryhill Burgh Halls and Glasgow Club Maryhill. Turn left along Gairbraid Avenue a short distance until you reach Maryhill Road (at W3W goals.civic.land). Turn right onto Maryhill Road and head in the direction of the town centre. Cross Maryhill Road at the pedestrian lights, and continue heading towards town. Soon you will reach the Viking Pub (at approx W3W using.live.trick), which is on the corner of Maryhill Road and Shakespeare Street. Turn left at the pub, along Shakespeare Street and past the McDonald's car park. On your right (at approx W3W maybe.descended.images) you will see the path that joins the canal path. Stay ahead and now follow the walk as described.

The distance walking on the road (pavement) is approximately half a mile (or 0.6 miles on the first option).

A short update on Claypits – There is a lot of work still to be done on the Claypits Local Nature Reserve, however at the time of writing this update/appendix, it is coming along quite well. We have updated Walk 6 to say that the new access bridge from Firhill has now been completed and is open for use. One of the paths is partially completed and a short "round trip" is possible by crossing at the new bridge (at approx W3W fruit.gross.combining) and turning left along the new path until it ends. At this point, you walk up and head along the pavement in front of the canal-side housing until you reach the road bridge at Firhill Road (at W3W bumps.spaces.tent). Cross the road bridge over the canal and rejoin the canal path (at W3W both.face.nurse). This will be easiest to navigate by doing it on your return, after visiting Speirs Wharf.

At the time of writing the Claypits entrance at Applecross Street was still closed and work was being done there.

We hope that you have enjoyed reading this mini guide and it has helped you to discover some enjoyable walks in and near Glasgow's west end.

If you can take the time to write a short review, we would be very grateful for the feedback.

Many thanks,

The Exploreourworld team.

Printed in Great Britain
by Amazon